Fingerprints

Kate Armstrong

WestBow
PRESS
A DIVISION OF THOMAS NELSON

WestBow Press books may be ordered through booksellers or by contacting:

WestBow Press
A Division of Thomas Nelson
1663 Liberty Drive
Bloomington, IN 47403
www.westbowpress.com
1-(866) 928-1240

Because of the dynamic nature of the Internet, any web addresses or links contained in this book may have changed since publication and may no longer be valid. The views expressed in this work are solely those of the author and do not necessarily reflect the views of the publisher, and the publisher hereby disclaims any responsibility for them.

Any people depicted in stock imagery provided by Thinkstock are models, and such images are being used for illustrative purposes only.

Certain stock imagery © Thinkstock.

ISBN: 978-1-4497-4987-3 (sc)
ISBN: 978-1-4497-4988-0 (e)

Library of Congress Control Number: 2012907596

Printed in the United States of America

WestBow Press rev. date: 05/08/2012

This is a true story about my life, a life that went
from being a victim to becoming a victor!

A portion of my story was broadcast on television to nearly every
nation on the planet. Now you can read it in its entirety for yourself.

I dedicate this book to my beloved grandmother, Oma Belle, and to my precious son, David Nathaniel. I am so privileged and honored to be the descendant of one and the mother of the other. They are two of the greatest examples of what it means to be a true follower of Jesus that I have ever known.

Contents

Acknowledgment

Belma Michael Johnson

Just a few hours with this man inspired me to bring my story to print. Thank you!

In Appreciation

I could not have completed this book if it weren't for my husband Michael. His many hours of hard work typing the manuscript were invaluable.

Preface

I WAS TERRIFIED. THE LARGE adult woman yelling at me was angry…very angry. She yanked the small ballerina figure from my hand, and then forcefully pulled me toward her. I instinctively knew that what was about to happen to me would hurt, and it would be far worse, and way beyond the norm of basic discipline. As she grabbed me, she quickly lifted my dress and pulled down my underwear, almost simultaneously. I began to cry.

Moments earlier, I had been alone in a bedroom that I was intrigued with, because it contained so many interesting things. One of my favorite things was a musical jewelry box. Every time I would lift the lid, a beautiful ballerina would stand and dance to a lovely tune. I had never seen anything like it before. I loved lifting the lid over and over, watching the little ballerina dance. I was also very interested in the mechanics of how it worked. After many times of opening and closing the lid, I decided to try and figure out how the lovely little ballerina could stand, and then lay down when the lid was closed. I pulled on the ballerina, and after some effort, she came out. It appeared that a rather large metal rod went through her, extending down below her feet. The end of the rod was pointed and sharp, like a large sewing needle.

I examined the little ballerina, and her appendage, for quite some time before deciding I should try and put her back in her proper place on top of the jewelry box. As I was attempting to put her back, I was caught unawares by the angry woman. She began to yell. I don't remember the words, just the tone of her voice.

Before I knew it, the sharp rod attached to the ballerina was being used as a tool to inflict pain in my body. It was pushed into the right cheek of my bottom. I screamed in pain and in horror. I tried to get away, but couldn't. After this horrible act of abuse was over, I pulled back to get as far from this woman as possible. I remember the feeling of the pain, not so much the physical pain, but the emotional pain in my heart. The woman I was staring at, while I cried huge tears, was now someone I feared. Before that moment, I had only feelings of love and trust for the angry woman, who now stood before me. I had believed that she would love me unconditionally, protect me, and nurture me. I was wrong. My innocent trust was crushed. My faith in her as my protector was betrayed. This was the very first act of betrayal that I have memory of. There would be many more to come. I was four.

It was summertime, I was nine years old. I have always looked much older than my actual age. I was taken by the angry woman to Las Vegas, Nevada. I didn't want to go with her. I would have preferred to stay at home with my beloved grandparents, whom I adored. As much as I cherished and adored them, they loved me infinitely more. My grandparents provided me with unconditional love, protection and the nurturing care that every child needs. They also provided me with all the wonderful material things I loved. I was their little princess. So there I was in Las Vegas with the angry woman; just the two of us. I refer to her as the angry woman, because she too often was just that, angry. She brought me with her, because she wanted me to spend time with her, and her new fiancé, who would be joining us in a day or so.

We checked into our hotel, and had a late lunch. After lunch, we decided to try out the hotel pool. We swam, and actually had a nice time. I started to think that maybe this trip would be a good trip. It was a little mini vacation. Maybe it would be fun.

We went back to our room and ordered room service for dinner. I turned the TV on and tried to find something of interest to watch. I also watched her, as she sat in front of a mirror and began to put her make-up on. Her primping took quite awhile. I wondered what she was planning. She said nothing to me about what her intentions were.

She was nearly finished getting herself ready, when she called me over to her. I got up, went over and sat down. She began to put make-up on me; eyeliner, mascara, lipstick and rouge. Then she started pulling my hair up and putting bobby-pins in my hair to keep it up. I asked her why she was doing all of these things to me, and she said that we would be going out.

I had never had any kind of make-up on before; after all, I was only nine years old. Now, after the application of make-up, I looked much older.

I had been to Las Vegas before with my grandparents and other family members. I had learned how to swim while vacationing there a few years before. I had always enjoyed our family trips to Vegas, but this trip was different. This trip was just me and the adult woman that I feared. I knew a drastic difference existed between how she thought of me, and how my grandparents thought of me. During those earlier Vegas trips I had only experienced Vegas during the daytime. I was about to enter a whole new world, Las Vegas at night.

We walked into a dimly lit bar. Terror gripped me, as I followed this woman into that bar. She led me to a table with four chairs around it. We sat down. In no time at all, two men came over and asked if they could join us. I was paralyzed with fear. I couldn't speak. Being in this situation took me back to when at the age of five or six; I had spent the weekend with the angry woman. She and her roommates were having one of their wild, loud and drunken parties. I was alone in a bedroom, lying there in the dark, trying to sleep, but it was impossible because of all the noise. The door opened, and a strange man that I had never seen before, came in and sat on my bed. He reeked of alcohol and cigarettes. Again, I was paralyzed with fear. I wanted to scream for help, but couldn't. He lay next to me and got his face just an inch or two from my face. He spoke about giving me money, and putting it under my pillow. I could hear everyone in the next room, yelling, screaming, laughing and dancing to the very loud music. No one came in to rescue me. This man tried to touch me, but I became angry and told him to leave. He did put money under my pillow, and told me not to say anything to anyone.

The men in the Vegas bar began to engage in conversation with us, and they ordered drinks for the table. One of the men began to speak to me exclusively, asking many personal questions. The angry woman mocked me for not answering the questions posed to me. They laughed and drank, and smoked cigarettes. The woman and her new male companion began to get very friendly with one another.. I continued to be paralyzed with fear, but tried to speak so that they wouldn't mock me and laugh at me any further. I have no idea how long this nightmare continued, but thankfully it did end. I was back in the hotel room in my bed, still very fearful, but so glad that the Vegas night life part of the ordeal was over. I remember thinking, that if I were to tell my grandmother what this woman did to me, she surely would have killed her. I never told anyone about that night…until now.

The woman's fiancé arrived in Vegas the next evening. He never knew his soon to be wife, had spent the previous evening with a strange man in a bar, drinking and acting like a harlot.

At the age of eighteen, I fell in love with a boy, who was my boss at the fast food restaurant where I worked. He was twenty. We began to date, and fell deeply in love. After about a year, we became engaged. He had been living at home with his parents and worked while he attended college. His dad was very angry about our engagement, because we were so young. His father gave him an ultimatum, either brake off the engagement or move out. My fiancé chose the latter. The problem was he had no place to go. The angry woman offered to let him move in with her. He did.

They began a secret affair that lasted for months, while he was engaged to me. She swore him to secrecy. He didn't honor that pledge, and told me everything. She had set a trap, and he fell in. At that time, I never would have believed that even she was capable of such betrayal. Some years later, she would also attempt to take my life by making and giving me poisoned iced tea. She failed.

What causes people to commit such evil against others? We read in the Bible, in the Book of Ephesians 6:12 it says, "For we do not wrestle against flesh and blood, but against principalities, against powers, against rulers of the darkness of this age, against spiritual hosts of wickedness in the heavenly places." This truth is what Jesus and His disciples knew very well. That is why they were able to easily forgive those who caused them harm and even death. Demons are very real, and actively use people to commit horrendous atrocities against others.

As you continue to read my story in the following chapters, you will see that I am no longer a victim, but a victor! I now pursue the true enemy, casting him out and setting the captives free…in Jesus' name!

Introduction

WE ALL HAVE STORIES TO tell—life stories that are as unique and individual to us as our very own fingerprints. When you lift your hand up and look at the very small space at the end of your fingers, it's hard to imagine that out of an estimated 7 billion people, not another person on the planet has the same fingerprints as you! In the Bible, Psalm 139:14 says, "I will praise you, for I am fearfully and wonderfully made; marvelous are your works, and that my soul knows very well."

You are about to read my story. There isn't another story quite like mine.

Chapter 1

In the Beginning

I was born to an unwed teenage mother. Thankfully, my birth occurred back before *Roe v. Wade* became law. Otherwise, I wouldn't be here now, writing this book. Gratefully, my maternal grandmother was a godly woman who took me right from the hospital and took complete care of me. My mother had considered putting me up for adoption, but my grandmother had told her that she would regret it. My grandmother told my mother that she would take care of me until my mother found a nice man to marry. Then, when she got settled, she could take me. My biological father was a married man and not in the picture.

My crib was in my grandmother's room. As soon as I began to speak, my grandmother would pray out loud every night and say the Lord's Prayer and the 23rd Psalm. When I was a child of eighteen months to a few years old, I would lie in my crib in my grandmother's room and recite those prayers with her every night. I don't have memory of anything else that far back, but hearing the word of God spoken out loud and then repeating it back was so powerful that I have vivid memory of that special time with my grandmother. Romans 10:17 says, "So then faith cometh by hearing, and hearing by the word of God." God had left His fingerprints on me. Through the power of His word, I knew God as a very young child. I have memory of intimacy with my heavenly Father as a baby! Psalm 27:10 says, "When my father and my mother forsake me, then the LORD will take care of me."

My life with my grandparents, who adored me, was really wonderful. I felt completely loved and protected by them. When I was nine years old, I was sent to live with another family member. I didn't want to leave my grandparents and the only home I knew, a home that was so loving and nurturing. My grandmother had health issues and high blood pressure, and she was concerned that she wouldn't be able to care for me any longer. I quickly went from being a very happy, well-adjusted child to a desperately depressed and suicidal child. My new environment was extremely abusive emotionally, mentally, and physically. It was clear that I was in a place that was very hostile, unloving, and void of any desire for my presence. I endured regular beatings, yelling, rage, and alcoholism. In my early teens, I was encouraged by an adult close to me to use drugs. I was told that he wanted to know what it was like. I never did use any drugs during that time. Looking back, I believe that the adult was trying to get me to use drugs so he would have an excuse to kick me out of their house. I had battles raging around me continually.

I was a built-in maid and babysitter. I was never permitted to go outside and play with friends after school. I was left alone with two small children for several hours every day. This went on for years. I never knew the names of any children on my block because I was never allowed to go out and play with them. I remember sitting by the window and watching kids play, wanting so desperately to join them.

At the age of thirteen, I heard the beautiful gospel message at a church winter youth camp, and I officially asked Jesus to be my Lord and take control of my life. Jesus became my savior that weekend. I was overjoyed. As soon as I got home, I told my family members of my conversion and trust in Jesus. One of them became enraged and angrily demanded that I never say the name of Jesus in their home again. The horrible spiritual, physical, emotional, and mental abuse by the family members escalated for the next four years. One family member came to me one night and told me to leave the house. He said he wouldn't call the police because I was a minor of seventeen. The next morning, I packed up my belongings, all that I could fit into my little two-seater car that I had purchased with savings that my grandmother had started for me when I was a baby. So there I was, out in the world, alone, without any support and no job, schooling, or money. I floundered and tried to live a Christian life, but sadly, I became immersed in the world with all its trappings: drugs, alcohol, and sexual encounters that produced four pregnancies—four precious children I chose to abort because that was the easy solution, or so I believed at that time. Jesus was definitely not the Lord of my life. I didn't allow Him to guide and direct my life. I had put him in the backseat with a gag over His mouth.

After ten years of living my life on my terms, I married a man who was not a Christian. He was an alcoholic, drug user, verbal abuser, and chain smoker. I had planned to leave him just months after we were married, but discovered I was pregnant. The marriage was a disaster. My husband, Michael, believed that he had made a huge mistake in marrying me, because he was always drunk. He thought his decision had been made under the influence of alcohol. After I had made one huge mistake after another during the ten years I had been living on my own, I decided that I needed and wanted Jesus to be in charge again. It is important to note here that in the course of the ten years I had lived on my own and made my own choices, many times I had repented and asked God to forgive me, a series of "rededications" that didn't last. So here I was now, wasting away in a horrible marriage and pregnant. Jeremiah 3:22 says, "Return, you backsliding children, and I will heal you of your backslidings. Indeed we do come to you, for you are the LORD our God." I cried out to God to please, once and for all, heal me of backsliding. God is faithful to His word! He did! That was the last time I ever had a problem with backsliding. It's interesting to note in that verse that God says He will heal you of *backslidings*, plural, and in His amazing love and grace, He still calls us children when we are living contrary to His Word and will. It is also very important to understand that there must be repentance and a complete change in behavior. Our lives must line up with God's Word, commandments, and laws. We must obey God's Word. Luke 6:46 says, "But why do you call me LORD, LORD and not do the things which I say?" In Mathew 7:21–3, He states, "Not everyone who says to me, LORD, LORD, shall enter heaven. Many will say to me in that day, LORD, LORD, have we not prophesied in your name, cast out demons in your name, and done many wonders in your name? And then I will declare to them, I never knew you; depart from me, you who practice lawlessness!" Clearly, God expects us to obey His laws.

I experienced a great deal of the pain and sorrow as a result of the wrong choices that people in authority over my life made, people who were not living in accordance with God's Word, the Bible. Honestly, my life was also devastated because of my own wrong choices, choices that were contrary to the Word of God.

My beloved grandmother went home to heaven when I was fifteen years old. When she left, I lost the only human being who spoke biblical truth into my life.

I decided to stay in my marriage and trust God to perform a miracle in our lives. I wanted better for my son than to come from a broken home. I prayed for my husband. Our marriage was so dysfunctional that I told Michael we either had to go to marriage counseling or church. He chose church! We attended for five years, and finally, while we were walking to the car after service one day, Michael told me that he believed and asked Jesus to be his Lord and Savior! He was baptized after that. He stopped drinking, stopped doing drugs, and stopped smoking. He was a brand new person! Everything began to improve, and we went forward with our lives, regularly attending church and enjoying our son and our lives.

Chapter 2

Heading into the Storm

It was the fall of 1994, a beautiful late-September day. The air was cool and crisp with a lot of sunshine, typical for California at that time of year. My husband, Michael, was meeting me at the doctor's office later that morning to have our second ultrasound. I was excited to have the ultrasound technician confirm that we were indeed having a girl. Michael just couldn't understand how I could "know" it was a girl. Our family would soon be complete with the addition of our new daughter to our two boys, who were two and eleven.

After I browsed through some parenting magazines in the waiting room of the doctor's office, the door opened, and my name was called. This being my third pregnancy, I knew the routine by now. I changed into my backless smock and waited in the ultrasound room with Michael. My belly was large and uncomfortable already. The technician came in and greeted us. So far, everything was *normal*.

Paula, the technician, squeezed that cold jelly like lubricant all over my burgeoning belly and began pressing the ultrasound wand over and around. Her face changed from pleasant to mildly horrified. I immediately sensed that there was a problem. Paula continued to press and move the instrument as she stared at the monitor. I asked, "Is something wrong?"

She said that she was going to ask the doctor to come in. She left the room, and as Michael and I looked at each other, not knowing what was happening, my thoughts were those of concern and uncertainty. Just a couple of years before this day, I had been pregnant and had lost a baby because of a miscarriage. My second pregnancy with my younger son had also been very traumatic and stressful. (I will explain what happened concerning that ordeal in the next chapter.) I understood and had experienced the pain of losing a dearly wanted child. I didn't have a lot of time to think about much else as Paula and our wonderful doctor came into the room. The doctor had delivered our first child, so I had compete faith and trust in his knowledge and experience. Paula began to push on my stomach again as the doctor studied the monitor. Both faces were expressionless. Before I could ask any questions, the doctor said, "Please get dressed and meet me in my office."

Michael and I sensed that the prognosis wasn't going to be good. After I questioned Paula, all I could get her to say was that she was very sorry. Our hearts sank, and a sickening feeling overwhelmed me. Michael and I entered the doctor's private office and sat down. He began to define the term "anencephalia," which is a *congenital absence of part or all of the brain.* I was in complete shock and disbelief. Impossible! As Michael and I stared at each other and tried to process this horrific information, the doctor began to immediately press us to schedule an abortion. Because of my age and the fact that I had high blood pressure and eclampsia, which is a form of toxemia during pregnancy, the doctor felt that abortion was the only course to take. Before we could respond, he raised his pen to schedule the "procedure."

Michael and I stared at each other in total disbelief. We were speechless.

After Michael and I stared at each other for a few moments, I felt a surge of power, boldness, and unwavering resolve. I looked squarely at the doctor and told him I appreciated his detailed explanation of what was happening inside my womb but there would be no "procedure" performed. I explained that God Almighty had put this child in me and He would decide if and when she would return to Him! The doctor's stare was expressionless, and as he processed what I had just told him, he began to tell me that the child would surely die in utero, causing great risk to my health, suggesting that it was most probable that I would have a stroke and quite possibly die. I wondered if there would be any end to this hellish nightmare I found myself in. I had been told by my prominent, well-respected doctor that there was a probability that I would have a stroke and possibly die, or I could choose to take the life of my child. Still, this was not a difficult decision for me, not even for one second. I once again firmly answered the doctor and said I respected his opinion and advice but I would not allow my child to be destroyed. This entire situation was in God's hands. I trusted Him! The doctor did his best to be respectful and not call me an idiot.

From the information in my health questionnaire, which I had filled out on the first office visit a few years before, the doctor knew that in my early youth, I had allowed doctors to kill and destroy four of my children, otherwise known as abortions—all precious babies that I had become pregnant with through rebellious, promiscuous behavior. In those days, I was completely self-centered, and having an abortion was just a way of taking care of a "problem." I believed the lie that "it" wasn't really a baby. After some years of maturity and education about child development in utero, I learned that the babies I carried had a heart, and their own blood, at Day 22 from conception, and I had also rededicated my life to the Lord Jesus Christ. Now, abortion was out of the question. I will never be able to adequately explain the guilt and remorse about the abortions I previously underwent. For so many years after my abortions, I suffered from deep depression to the point of reoccurring suicidal thoughts and a couple of halfhearted attempts. What my doctor didn't know as I sat in his office that day and listened to him give me the prognosis was the depth of the pain, remorse, depression, and guilt I had endured for many years because of those abortions. I knew that I would never again allow one of my precious babies to be slaughtered in my womb, even if it cost me my own life. Michael was in complete agreement with me.

The weeks went by, and I enjoyed every minute of my pregnancy. We named our daughter Makenna Ariel, which means *"head lioness of God."* Interestingly, her name was chosen before the diagnosis of anencephalia. Makenna grew and moved and pressed her little feet out against my womb. I could feel the heels of her feet as she stretched. Fall turned into winter. We enjoyed Christmas 1994 with our two active and healthy boys, and on January 10, 1995, I went into labor and delivered our precious Makenna Ariel, our head lioness of God, who was missing most of the back of her head. She took one breath, and when the umbilical cord was cut, she went into the loving, receiving arms of God. Labor had been very difficult, and my blood pressure had risen quite high because it had been a vaginal delivery that lasted for several hours. My boys had both been C-sections.

The doctor had been kind enough to place my most precious, almost perfect, six-pound daughter into a bassinet next to my bed. That time to grieve and say good-bye was precious. Because of the condition of Makenna's skull, my bladder had been damaged by exposed bone tearing it as she was coming down the birth canal. The doctor did what he could to repair my bladder, but there was continual bleeding. The doctor couldn't get the bleeding to stop, so he told me that I would need to go in for emergency bladder surgery … right now.

The whole ordeal had been mentally and physically draining for both me and Michael. Michael went home to be with our boys, so I was left alone for surgery to repair my bladder. I was devastated, and I really thought that my body wouldn't be able to take any more trauma. I fully believed that I would die during surgery. Fear had a firm hold on me.

When I awoke, I was alone, and I was in great pain spiritually, physically, mentally, and emotionally. Within the past seven hours, I had delivered a baby, who had passed away, and I had endured surgery to repair my bladder during hormonal, emotional, mental, and spiritual upheavals. My breasts were so swollen and painful, ready to nurse a child I didn't have. I began to cry and couldn't stop.

A few days later, I was released from the hospital. I had a catheter attached to me now that would remain inside of me for eight weeks until my bladder had healed. Michael picked me up from the hospital. I was very weak from the trauma my body had endured, but the mental and emotional devastation was much greater. I hadn't eaten anything in the days after the delivery and could only take two to three steps before I would need to rest. After Michael and I left the hospital, we immediately stopped at the cemetery to make funeral arrangements. Then we went to the florist to order flowers. I wore a long dress to cover the urine bag attached to my leg.

We conducted the funeral, and many attended, including Paula, the ultrasound technician who spoke very kindly about how I had comforted her after we had gotten the news from the doctor in his office that fall day that now seemed so long ago. We put our little angel in the ground. Surely, that would be the end of our horrific devastation … wouldn't it? We put January 10, 1995, behind us as best we could. After all, we had two wonderful boys to raise and enjoy.

Chapter 3

David Nathaniel Armstrong

I ABSOLUTELY LOVE WHAT NAMES mean. Every time I discovered I was pregnant, I would get out one of my three name definition books. Our first son came to me one day when he was about seven and said, "Mama, I really want a brother." He didn't know it, but we had been trying for years. I had a miscarriage just a couple of years before, but despite that setback, we were actively trying to have another child.

I said, "Great. Let's pray together and ask God to give you a brother." And so we prayed.

About a year later, during Christmas 1991, I found out that we were pregnant. Of course I already knew it would be a boy. That was what we had prayed for! We were all very excited that a second child would be coming into our family.

Three to four months into the pregnancy, I scheduled my first office visit. There were routine tests performed, including blood tests. A few days later, the doctor called me to give me the test results. When a doctor begins a call with "I'm very sorry," that's your cue to sit down. "Mrs. Armstrong, the results show that your baby has Down syndrome. I'm very sorry. Would you like to speak to my nurse about scheduling an abortion?"

After a few moments of silence, I said, "No, thank you, Doctor. God put this child in my womb, and He will decide how He wants to create him.

Besides, we know that God still heals and performs miracles every day. We will pray and ask God to perform a miracle."

Later that day, everyone in our church knew about the doctor's call and what the doctor had said. Our prayer request went out all over the church. People everywhere were praying. We kept praying. Spring of 1992 had come and gone, and I was heading into summer with what had to have been the largest stomach a pregnant woman has ever had with only one child! It was hot, and I was large and miserable.

During all the office visits and tests that were done, the doctor's diagnosis remained the same. The one test result that gave us all great joy was that we were truly having a boy! My oldest son was so excited about his new baby brother. He caught my enthusiasm about names and what they meant. He and I looked through my name books together. He said, "Mama, how about David? I really like that name." (I found that David meant *beloved*) Surely, this child was that already. It was discussed within the family, and then we decided. David would be his name. Now we needed to choose just the right middle name to express how grateful we all were about his life and what he already meant to us. I chose Nathaniel, which meant *"gift of God,"* Perfect. And so it was. Michael totally agreed.

At the end of the summer, my due date was quickly approaching. We were ready. The nursery was ready. Over the course of the previous months, I had told everyone that we trusted God to perform a miracle. We wanted a completely healthy baby from the top of his head to the bottom of his toes, as every parent would. Ultimately, we trusted God with whatever He wanted to do.

I was scheduled for a C-section on September 2, 1992. We rose before dawn to head to the hospital. It was dark, and I remember being excited, like it was Christmas morning, and I would open my present from my heavenly Father. The nurses were bustling about prepping me and then wheeling me into delivery. I opted for a local anesthesia. I wanted to be fully awake and coherent when my precious gift of God entered the world. After some time and pressure, out came my large nine-pound-nine-ounce baby boy. The doctors and nurses were silent. I looked at Michael for some indication of what was happening. Someone said that the baby wasn't breathing! And then … there was a loud cry! The doctor said that the boy had some sort of rash and blisters. They began to perform tests, and they put drops in his eyes. As I lay there, I wondered if anyone was going to tell me if he was fine. Finally, it was declared that David Nathaniel Armstrong was perfectly healthy, other than his strange rash! No Down syndrome! But because of the rash and blisters, they wanted to keep him in ICU for several days and watch him. They did, and Michael and I went to visit and hold him everyday. I nursed him during my hospital stay and the few days after I was released. Finally, after about a week, we were able to bring our precious baby home and become a family of four. Thank God we trusted Him. God performed a miracle!

Chapter 4

Life Is Perfect

SO THERE WE WERE, A family of four with two boys, one a newborn and the other a nine-year-old. We were living in Mission Viejo, California. Mission Viejo has a great little league program. We had started our oldest boy in T-ball when he was five and had enjoyed watching him play and progress every year. There is also a beautiful lake there in town where boats can be rented out. There are a lot of trees that change color in the fall so that the place looks a lot like New England but on a smaller scale. The homes are also designed like quaint Cape Cod homes with white picket fences. Our home was up on a hill overlooking the baseball field, lake, and trees. On the Fourth of July, they shot off fireworks from the lake. All we had to do was put up lawn chairs in our backyard and watch the festivities. The sights and sounds and smells of that area are things that are still very fresh in my mind. It was a Norman Rockwell-like life, complete with our two adorable brown dachshunds—a female named Wilhelmina (Willi for short) and the male named Arnie. Life was full of joy. We enjoyed baseball games, bicycle rides, cub scouts, swimming lessons, church activities, and neighborhood activities. Everything was perfect.

In the spring of 1993, we were able to buy a very large home in the seaside community of San Clemente, California, one that Michael's company had developed and built. Michael was the project manager, and he had personally overseen the construction of our dream home. It was absolutely the perfect place to raise a family. A gate guarded enclave of fifty homes high on a hill. We could now add surf lessons to our oldest son's list of activities.

We did a lot of entertaining for family and friends, regularly hosting barbecues, dinner parties, brunches, and weekly get-togethers. The house was always filled with children's chatter and the smells of freshly baked apple pies, chicken fettuccini with garlic, hot apple cider, and cinnamon. Christmas was always a huge deal. I loved all the smells at Christmastime. I was the happiest I had ever been. Everything in my life really seemed perfect. The pain and sorrow of losing Makenna and the concern and challenges of what we had experienced with my pregnancy with David were now all behind us. We had everything we wanted and needed. We had beautiful material possessions, two healthy, wonderful boys, and friends and family we regularly enjoyed. Financially, we had done well and were able to buy a thirty-four-foot powerboat. Michael's family had had boats when he had been growing up, and his dream was to have his own. We were out on our boat nearly every weekend, taking wonderful family trips to Catalina and up and down the California coast, where we were able to get close to pods of whales. We also took many fishing trips when I would inevitably lose all our best lures. There was constantly a fun activity happening. Life was really good day after day and year after year until—

Chapter 5

August 19, 1996

THAT DATE AND THE DAYS and years after that day were so extremely difficult, so painful that I literally had to put writing this book on hold for fourteen years.

It was Monday morning. We had just celebrated Michael's birthday the day before. I was cleaning up from the party in addition to my usual Monday morning routine of house cleaning and laundry. I was trying to get as much done as possible before I took David to the pediatrician for his regular checkup. I wanted to put David in preschool as we had done for our oldest son. Preschool was great in helping prepare for kindergarten. The Christian school that our oldest attended needed a doctor's release for David, one showing that he was healthy and ready for school.

David was turning four on September 2, and school would start just days after that. I put my little man in his car seat and drove the few short blocks to the doctor's office. David asked me if he would be getting a shot. He actually looked forward to the injections, just as I did as a child, because after the shot, there would be a reward of a Tootsie Pop. I told him I didn't know but I didn't think so. David's name was called, and we went into the office. The pediatrician had been our doctor for both our kids. He was well known because of the numerous books he had written on parenting. The doctor greeted David with a smile, picked him up, and laid him on the exam table. The doctor asked me the usual questions about how David was doing as he pushed and probed David's abdomen. (I always wondered why doctors did that.) I answered that everything was fine, all normal. The doctor continued to probe, and after a few minutes without saying much more, he looked at me and said, "I want you to take David over to the hospital and have an ultrasound done of his abdomen." He spoke these words with complete calm like we had been having a friendly conversation about the weather. Before I could ask any questions, the doctor said, "I believe David has a Wilms' tumor. When I did my residency at a children's hospital for four years, these were primarily the cases I worked with."

Wait! What? Wilms' tumor? What is that? What does this mean?

The doctor said, "Go ahead and take David over for the ultrasound. And if I'm correct, come back, and we'll talk."

My heart was filled with so many feelings. It was hard to breathe. I felt anguish, dread, and deep concern for my precious son. He was only three years old, and the thought of him having to go through any tests at all was nearly unbearable to me. I so desperately wanted to protect him from all pain and discomfort. I didn't want anyone to touch him. Suddenly, thoughts of the past few years came rushing back. Everything I had tried to put behind me came back. All the pain and sorrow of the last few years was back, front and center. *Please, please, Father, no more heartache and devastation.*

The nurse had called ahead to the hospital to tell them we were coming right over for the ultrasound. The drive was short, and we were taken right into the exam room. The ultrasound was done, and we were told to go back to the pediatrician's office. I was thankful that everyone had communicated well with each other, giving me step-by-step directions and instructions about what to do and where to go. I was having a difficult time. Back at the pediatrician's office, the doctor's nurse led me to his private office. A short time later, the doctor came in. He gazed at me with a kind and sympathetic look, sat down, and began to tell me that the ultrasound showed that David did indeed have a Wilms' tumor. I sat there in quiet shock, not saying a word, waiting to hear the rest of this completely unwelcome news. I thought, *This can't be happening!* Wilms' tumor is a rare cancer that primarily affects children. Also known as nephroblastoma, Wilms' tumor is the most common cancer of the kidneys in children, and it often affects children age three to four and becomes much less common after age five. The outlook for most children with Wilms' tumor is very good. There's a 90 percent survival rate at the time of the diagnosis. After the doctor explained this disease, he looked at me and said, "Don't worry, Mrs. Armstrong. Of all the cancers, this is the best one to fight."

I knew his statement was meant to encourage me, but it didn't. Just nineteen months earlier, we had buried our precious daughter, and before that, we had endured a miscarriage. Then there had been that horrible emergency bladder surgery and those years of deep sorrow. I had endured three traumatic pregnancies that had caused me great stress and depression. We had fought hard to put all of that devastation behind us and move forward with the idyllic life we so desperately wanted. I didn't want any part of this! The doctor said that David would have to have surgery to remove his kidney and then he would need chemotherapy. He would call a doctor he knew at Childrens Hospital of Orange County (CHOC). We needed to begin as soon as possible.

I don't remember the drive home. It was late afternoon by this time, and I waited for Michael to get home from work. This was something so monumental and devastating that he had to be told in person in the sanctuary of our home, not over the phone. David went to play in his room, and I just sat, going over all that I had been told that awful day. There wouldn't be any dinner cooked that night. No phone calls answered. Just silence … along with the quiet, angelic sounds of a three-year-old playing make-believe in his room.

As I sat in our family room and looked outside into our big beautiful backyard with the lovely view of the hills and large estates in the distance, I wondered how I could possibly endure this next valley of uncertainty. The sun was setting behind the lush green hills when Michael came home. How do you prepare someone for the horrific storm that you know is going to devastate them? Michael has always been a pretty easygoing, upbeat man. After I gave him all the information and details I could remember, I watched his happy, smiling face change into a shocked, deeply saddened expression of disbelief. The color drained from his face, and all he could say over and over was "no, no, no." Tears filled our eyes as we both sat in silence.

I got up sometime in the middle of the night and stood in the doorway of David's room. The room was dimly lit from a nightlight. I stood there, staring at my beautiful, precious, perfect little boy soundly sleeping in his bed, completely unaware that his mama, who adored him, stood in the shadows with tears flowing so heavily that her vision was blurred. *The heaves of my chest and gasps of air are sure to wake him*, I thought. I stood there a very long time, crying out to God to perform a miracle. I couldn't stand the thought of my baby going into surgery and being cut open. If only I could take his place, I would gladly volunteer a thousand times over.

We slept very little that night. The next day was lovely, a warm day. We threw out whatever plans we had that day and decided to go to the beach as a family. I watched my little boy play in the water, running from the waves, making mounds of sand he called forts. We had spoken to the doctor at CHOC that morning, and the exam, test, and surgery had been scheduled for later that week. I wanted David to play in the water that he loved because I knew it would be a long time before he would be able to again.

Kate at 3 with Beloved Grandparents

Michael and Kate Newly Married

Our Brand New Dream Home in San Clemente

Our Boat.

Our First Born Steven with His Beloved Willi

Our Wonderful Boys 1993

David Age 2 Before Diagnosis

David at 5 September 1997

David and Dad

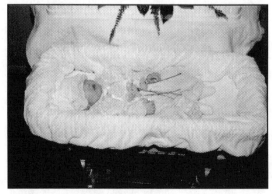

Our Precious McKenna Ariel

Beach Day After Diagnosis

David sleeping the night after seeing the pediatrician

David at amusement park September 1997

Chapter 6

I Didn't Know Valleys Could Be So Deep

FROM THE TIME WE KNEW the surgery date through the entire ordeal of four more surgeries and months of chemotherapy, I barely existed. This was such a living hell for all of us that words can never adequately explain the constant feelings of sadness, depression, and helplessness. In an effort to cope, my mind shut down. The pain and sorrow was so intense that my mind literally seemed to operate in a diminished state. I became very forgetful. I would often forget my purse or keys, leaving them in restaurants or on top of my car. Thinking back on those years is like looking back through a very thick mist and only remembering a few details.

Our precious David Nathaniel went through the initial surgery, at which time the surgeon removed his kidney and gallbladder. He then had another surgery to place a shunt into his heart so that the chemo drugs could be given to him through that. We were responsible for keeping the shunt as sterile as possible. We were told that infection was very likely and that any infection could require more surgeries to replace the shunts. Thankfully, David never needed another surgery because of any infection. The medical staff was amazed by that. We were told that they weren't aware of any child who did not need additional surgery for that issue. I had one job, and that was to take care of my baby the very best way possible. The thought of David having to endure another surgery because I didn't keep everything clean was … unthinkable. I won't go into greater detail here except to say that David had a total of five surgeries and chemo for about one year at two different hospitals. We battled and fought for fifteen months. The 90 percent success rate wasn't on our side. In November 1997, just days before Thanksgiving, our beloved gift of God went home to heaven. David had just turned five in September.

The cancer had moved into his lungs, and it had spread rapidly. After his last stem cell treatment, he looked up at me, and for the first time ever in all the months of pain, surgeries, and suffering, he said "Please, Mama, make them stop. They're torturing me!"

I tried to never cry in front of him, but after I heard those words, I broke down, which made him feel worse. He felt responsible for making me sad, and he tried to comfort me. The anguish at that moment was indescribable. The doctors wanted to keep trying other treatments. What the doctors didn't know was that a few years before David's birth, God had spoken to my heart and told me that He was going to take David home to heaven. In His great mercy and kindness, God allowed me to know His plan before it became a reality. I knew that no matter what we did and how hard we fought, God's plans and purposes were higher than ours. We were created by Him, and for Him, to love and worship Him, and to obey and trust Him … often when we don't understand His will, purpose, or plan. As a mother, it was devastating for me to release my precious little boy into eternity. I so desperately wanted to guard and protect him as I had whenever he had had surgery or chemo in the hospital. David was never alone. Either I or Michael or a family member stayed and slept in his room. Someone was with him continually, guarding, protecting, and watching everything.

The last week of David's life here on Earth, I tried to prepare him for his return home. He and I both had a difficult time with this. He didn't want to leave me. He said, "No, Mama, I don't want to go. I'll miss you too bad." He was holding on to this life through great pain and agony to his little body.

I couldn't bear seeing him fight for every breath of air he took, and I couldn't bear him not being with me here in this life. A few nights before he went home to heaven, I cried out to God and said, "Father, please give me some sign that David will be okay and happy."

The next day, David and I talked. I told him who would be there in heaven with him. Besides being with Father God and his Lord Jesus, he would be with his maternal great-grandmother and his beautiful sister. He refused to go, telling me over and over that he couldn't leave because he would "miss me too bad."

David was on oxygen and a morphine drip. Every breath he took was so much work for his little body. We had him in the living room on the sofa where many friends and family members filled every available space. David was very lucid. He interacted with everyone in the room and carried on coherent conversation the best he could, given how difficult it was for him to breathe. He even managed to sing our special song with me, "Blessed Assurance," which David and I sang together often during the fifteen months of his treatment. We all spent the entire day visiting with my beloved gift of God. During David's fifteen months of treatment, all he ever wanted was to go to the park and play. He loved swinging on the swings. At the very end of the afternoon, I was seated on the sofa next to him, and he looked straight ahead and said, "Mama, I want to go with those people and play!"

I said, "Do you see people playing?"

He said, "Yes."

I said, "You go, baby. Go play, and I'll be with you in a little while."

David breathed his last breath and went with those already in heaven to play. In His grace and mercy, God let me know where David was headed and what he would be doing. Thank you, Father.

We were fortunate to have the son of a world-renowned evangelist officiate David's service. It was pouring rain that day, and the church was standing room only. The gospel was preached, and the most amazing, loving gift of God in the form of an invitation was given to accept Jesus. We had salvations that day, including a couple of elderly Jewish friends. Our beloved David brought souls, precious souls into the kingdom of heaven with him. God moved in a powerful way that day, touching many lives in different ways. We had an open coffin, and David looked completely healthy. He really looked as though he was just sleeping. He radiated light and health! The glory of God was on him!

We buried our cherished son near his sister in the same cemetery. A few close friends and family joined us at the grave site. As I watched the attendants lower David's little coffin into the ground and begin to cover it with the dirt that had just been dug up that morning, I thought about how this had been my darling David Nathaniel, my beloved gift of God, my seed. What happens when seed is put into the ground and covered with dirt? In most instances, the person who places seed into the ground is a farmer who expects a harvest. At that moment I saw a much bigger plan. I prayed and said, "Father, I have once again put my precious seed into the ground, and now Father I ask you for a huge harvest of souls; like for like, allow me to be a farmer of souls in your harvest field—the Earth. Please allow me to have a huge harvest of souls!" Psalm 126:5–6 says, "Those who sow in tears shall reap in joy. He who continually goes forth weeping, bearing seed for sowing, shall doubtless come again with rejoicing, bringing his sheaves with him." Galatians 6:7 says, "Do not be deceived, God is not mocked; for whatever a man sows, that he will also reap." 2 Corinthians 9:6 says, "But this I say: He who sows sparingly will also reap sparingly, and he who sows bountifully will also reap bountifully."

After a miscarriage and putting two of my three children into the ground, I saw the planting of two of my children into the ground as a bountiful sowing. Genesis 26:12 says, "Then Isaac sowed in that land and reaped in the same year a hundredfold, and the LORD blessed him." There are some very powerful lessons here. First, there are many references in the Old Testament and the New Testament about obedience to God's laws and commandments. God is very clear about the consequences of disobedience and the blessings for obeying his laws and commandments. The seventh commandment is "You shall not murder," which can be found in the book of Deuteronomy. I allowed four of my precious babies to be slaughtered, murdered in my womb when I was a young girl living a life completely outside of the will of God. There are serious, painful consequences when you disobey God's Word. Believe me, I know. When you become a Christian by repenting and asking and trusting Jesus to forgive you of all your sin, He does. But that doesn't mean that you are then permitted to continue in willful sin. If you do, there will be consequences of discipline, and possibly judgment. I became a Christian at thirteen and read my Bible. I knew deep in my heart that abortion was murder, but at the time, I believed God would just overlook my rebellion. He didn't. Galatians 6:7 says "Do not be deceived, God is not mocked, for whatever a man sows, that he will also reap." I brought punishment on myself due to my rebellion. Committing four abortions equaled one miscarriage and two children, whom I adored and wanted with all my heart, buried in the ground. And then my dear firstborn son, who had been raised in a Christian home, educated in Christian schools, decided at the age of eighteen that he doubted the existence of God. His decision broke my heart. But in spite of his declaration, I also knew that God performs His word, and the day will come when my son will proclaim that Jesus is his Lord. Deuteronomy 30:6 says, "And the LORD your God will circumcise your heart and the heart of your descendants, to love the LORD your God with all your heart and with all your soul, that you may live." I stand on all of God's promises, which are bountiful and generous to those who trust and believe and obey His Word.

For your own sake and for your good, please stay rooted in God's Word, the Bible. Read it. Study it. Memorize it. Obey it. From what I have been told by biblical scholars who are much more knowledgeable that I am, the King James Version is the most accurate to the original transcripts. I use the New King James because it is easier to read; it's the only one I use. Bibles are now being rewritten to accommodate lifestyles, having little to do with God's original Holy Spirit-inspired Word. Many modern translations omit a lot of Scripture from the original transcripts. By knowing God's word and obeying it, you will be kept from making horrible life changing choices.

During that time, I found out that there was no valley so deep that the loving arms of Jesus couldn't reach deeper still in order to hold and comfort someone. I also discovered that the precious Holy Spirit is truly the perfect comforter.

Another very important lesson I learned concerned the power of forgiveness. To forgive can be a very difficult decision to make, especially given the degree of the offense you are trying to forgive. I completely understand. I didn't speak to a very close relative for ten years because of a horrible betrayal from that family member. That offense along with more pain caused by that person put me in a state of rage for many years. Sadly, when this happens, you are the one in the emotional prison and bondage. In addition to what I just mentioned, that rage can lead to more destructive behaviors, both to you and to others. You open a door to the enemy to come into your life and to do as he desires—to rob, kill, and destroy you and others. Mark 11:26 says, "But if you do not forgive, neither will your

Father in Heaven forgive your trespasses." This is very serious! I heard the testimony of a pastor from Africa who said that he had had a terrible argument with his wife. After several hours of verbally abusing each other, she apologized and asked him to forgive her. The pastor remained angry and refused her apology. The next day, he was driving on a difficult road and crashed his car. He died in that crash and found himself in hell. He called out to the LORD and was told that because of his unforgiveness toward his wife, he would now spend eternity in hell. The pastor began to plead with the LORD and stated his case. He said that he was a pastor and had served God for years. The pastor pleaded for mercy and found himself back in his body. In His great love and mercy, God allowed the pastor to return. The pastor had a huge attitude adjustment and tells everyone he can about his experience.

For me, I began one day to pray and ask God to forgive me for all the hatred, rage, bitterness, and unforgiveness in my heart toward those who had hurt me so badly. The absolute victory and breakthrough came the day I prayed, "Father, I forgive them, and I ask you to forgive them and not hold anything against them on my account." Breakthrough! The Holy Spirit came in like a flood and saturated me with love, forgiveness, joy, and peace. We have now learned that many infirmities are rooted in unforgiveness and unrepented sin.

Through forgiveness, there is peace, healing, and deliverance from depression, remorse, and suicidal thoughts. You might be reading this right now and suffering with these issues. The LORD wants to set you completely free from this bondage. He absolutely loves you, and He wants to forgive you, but you must get real with Him about your sins. I prayed and begged God to forgive me with tears streaming down my face, but I still suffered with depression due to the abortions. I eventually confessed what I had done in the past to another person, and she sweetly and lovingly prayed with me because she had also had an abortion in her youth. When I brought my skeletons out of the closet, confessed, and prayed with another person, I was set free. In James 5:16, we read, "Confess your trespasses to one another, and pray for one another, that you may be healed. The effective, fervent prayer of a righteous man avails much." Also, 1 John 1:9 says, "If we confess our sins, He is faithful and just to forgive us our sins and to cleanse us from all unrighteousness." I wasn't able to get release from the bondage as long as I kept the secret of my abortions in the closet. My image was too important to me. I didn't want anyone to think badly of me or judge me. Proverbs 28:13 says, "He who covers his sins will not prosper, but whoever confesses and forsakes them will have mercy." I can say a big amen to that!

There are countless numbers of women in churches suffering great pain in regards to the abortion issue. Jesus doesn't want you to spend one more day in pain and bondage. There will be those who will judge you. Don't worry about that for one second. They either have never experienced the love of God in their lives or have forgotten just how much God has forgiven them of all their sins. I promise you that the freedom and peace you will experience will far outweigh any judgment someone might level against you.

Chapter 7

Victory!

THE PURPOSE OF THIS BOOK is first and foremost to bring glory, honor, and praise to Almighty God, my Father, and to Jesus, my Lord and Savior. The other purpose of this book is to help all who read my story to learn from my mistakes. Hopefully, you will make all the correct choices based on the Word of God, which is our life manual. John 17:17 says, "Sanctify them by Your truth, Your word is truth." God's word is absolutely true from cover to cover. Obey it, and you will have all of God's blessings contained in His word. That's His promise. I didn't write this book to give you some "feel good" message promising that once you become a Christian, everything will be wonderful beyond words and you'll never have problems. That message sounds great, but it is totally wrong. The Scripture I used as a guide in writing this book and how I live my life is based on 2 Timothy 4:1–5, which says the following:

> I charge you therefore before God and the Lord Jesus Christ, who will judge the living and the dead at His appearing and His kingdom! Preach the word! Be ready in season and out of season. Convince, rebuke, exhort, with all longsuffering and teaching. For the time will come when they will not endure sound doctrine, but according to their own desires, because they have itching ears, they will heap up for themselves teachers; and they will turn their ears away from the truth, and be turned aside to

fables. But you be watchful in all things, endure afflictions, do the work of an evangelist, fulfill your ministry!

Another very important scripture that guides my life is John 4:24. It says, "God is spirit, and those who worship Him must worship in spirit and truth." There is nothing hidden in my life anymore. Truth, transparency, and accountability are the principals guiding my life.

It is not a pleasant thing to open yourself up and expose all the terrible things you have done in your life. How can I tell you how great God is in His amazing love, grace, and forgiveness if I don't tell you exactly how horrible I was? In addition to the abortions, hatred, unforgiveness, and rebellion, I committed adultery twice early in my marriage. In my youth, I was engaged in nearly every sin imaginable. My life was completely out of control. Friends who have known me for only the last few years can't imagine I had been the horrible person I was. Exactly my point! In His indescribable love, God forgives you when you repent, and He makes you brand new! I am not the person I once was. I am a new creation! Second Corinthians 5:17 says, "Therefore, if anyone is in Christ, he is a new creation; old things have passed away; behold, all things have become new." I have enough life experience to tell you that God is great! And Jesus is Lord! Luke 1:37 says, "For with God nothing will be impossible." First Corinthians 12:3 says, "Therefore I make known to you that no one speaking by the Spirit of God calls Jesus accursed, and no one can say that Jesus is LORD except by the Holy Spirit."

During my life, I have dealt with intense hatred, rage, and unforgiveness toward people in authority in my life , and I didn't speak to them for ten years because of choices in behavior they chose that drastically affected me so negatively, that I spoke of in the Preface and in Chapter One. I suffered for more than twenty-five years with horrendous guilt, remorse, sadness, depression, suicidal thoughts, and suicide attempts because of four abortions. I've endured deep valleys of inexplicable pain, sorrow, and loss because of a miscarriage and the passing of two of my children, not to mention a difficult relationship with my only surviving child. I am closely acquainted with sorrow and devastation. The devil comes to kill and destroy. He certainly caused havoc in my life for far too long. God is more than capable of turning what Satan intends for evil into something good! The Lord God has done just that for me and countless others. I have been completely set free from all hatred, unforgiveness, depression, suicidal thoughts, guilt, and more by the love, grace, and mercy of God through Jesus, His Son, my savior and Lord! John 8:36 says, "Therefore if the Son makes you free, you shall be free indeed." John 10:10 says, "The thief does not come except to steal, and to kill, and to destroy. I have come that they may have life, and that they may have it more abundantly." I am a brand new person. All of my broken relationships have been restored, and many acts of love and kindness have been demonstrated to me by my family members over time. God has opened doors for me to proclaim His greatness to the world. I now have the privilege and honor of telling the world through my healing and evangelistic ministry that God is great! And Jesus is Lord! God's love and arms are open to you now. He longs to have a relationship with you and make you His child. I urge you to make the best decision you could ever make for yourself. Pray a simple prayer from your heart to God. Repent of your sins, everything that you have done or said that was contrary to God's laws and commandments.

The following scripture references are extremely important to read and to understand:

1 Corinthians 6:8–11 says, "No, you yourselves do wrong and cheat, and you do these things to your brethren! Do you not know that the unrighteous will not inherit the Kingdom of God? Do not be deceived. Neither fornicators, nor idolaters, nor adulterers, nor homosexuals, nor sodomites, nor thieves, nor covetous, nor drunkards, nor revilers, nor extortioners will inherit the Kingdom of God. And such were some of you. But you were washed, but you were sanctified, but you were justified in the name of the LORD JESUS and by the Spirit of our God."

Revelation 21:8 says, "But the cowardly, unbelieving, abominable, murders, sexually immoral, sorcerers, idolaters, and all liars shall have their part in the lake which burns with fire and brimstone, which is the second death."

Mathew 7:21–23 says, "Not everyone who says to me, LORD, LORD, shall enter Heaven, but he who does the will of my Father in Heaven. Many will say to me in that day, LORD, LORD, have we not prophesied in your name, cast out demons in your name, and done many wonders in your name? And then I will declare to them, I never knew you; depart from me, you who practice lawlessness!" We must obey; obey God's laws and commandments!

Jesus speaks in Mathew 19:17: "But if you want to enter into life, keep the commandments."

Tell God you are sorry and ask Jesus to be your Lord and savior. Ask Jesus to take charge of your life from now on and change your behavior. Read your Bible daily and obey it. Find godly leaders who preach and teach the uncompromised Word of God without apology. Find a good Bible-based church and attend every Sabbath.

I cannot emphasize enough how horrible eternal hell will be for those who are unrepentant. Let's examine what God says about hell: Psalm 55:15 says, "Let death seize them; let them go down alive into Hell. For wickedness is in their dwellings and among them." Jesus says in Mathew 13:49 and 50, "So it will be at the end of the age. The angels will come forth, separate the wicked from among the just, and cast them into the furnace of fire. There will be wailing and gnashing of teeth." Jesus also says in Mathew 25:46, "And these will go away into everlasting punishment, but the righteous into eternal life." Revelation 20:15 states, "And anyone not found written in the book of life was cast into the Lake of Fire." And finally, Revelation 20:10 says, "The devil, who deceived them, was cast into the Lake of Fire and Brimstone where the beast and the false prophet are. And they will be tormented day and night forever and ever."

In hell, you will burn in indescribable heat and fire with no escape. You will thirst continually without water. The stench of burning flesh and brimstone will never leave your nostrils. You will stay in complete darkness forever. You will scream in desperate agony and pain without end. You will hear the screams and bloodcurdling cries of millions of souls who surround you. You will spend every second of your existence for the rest of eternity remembering how you didn't have to be there. You will remember how God reached out to you, the times He invited you to repent and receive Jesus as your Lord and Savior. In your pride and rebellion, you rejected the one and only way to escape such indescribable horror. In His great love and mercy, God is asking you again right now. Repent! Ask God to forgive you and ask Jesus to wash all of your sins away by His priceless blood.

Jesus says in John 14:6, "I am the way, the truth, and the life. No one comes to the Father except through me."

Chapter 8

Love or Hate?

As was previously mentioned in the last chapter, there will be many people who will not enter into heaven. Many say that anyone who believes such things is a narrow-minded, intolerant bigot. Let's examine this way of thinking. There must be a place where people draw from as a source of truth. I maintain that absolute truth is God's word, the Bible. The Bible has proven itself historically, scientifically, and prophetically. In the book of John 17:17, it says, "Sanctify them by your truth. Your word is truth." Psalm 119:142 says, "Your righteousness is an everlasting righteousness, and your law is truth." Psalm 33:4 says, "For the word of the LORD is right, and all His work is done in truth." Psalm 119:160 says, "The entirety of your word is truth and every one of your righteous judgments endures forever." There are many more Scripture references declaring the Bible as truth.

There are those, myself included, who actively speak out and tell everyone who will listen about the Word of God, His laws, and His commandments. Why? Because those of us who have been utterly transformed by God's love through Jesus Christ don't want anyone to go to hell. There are no words to adequately express how terrible hell is. It's eternally horrific. John 3:16 says, "For God so loved the world that He gave His only begotten Son, that whoever believes in Him should not perish but have everlasting life." Jesus said in Mathew 4:17, "Repent for the Kingdom of Heaven is at hand."

If you believe that warning people of what their futures will be like without Jesus as their Lord and Savior, is narrow minded, bigoted hate speech, then consider the following illustration:

There were two women walking down the street, one on each side of the street. The women were from the town and knew the area very well. They were both heading in the same direction into town. Imagine this situation was set within a small mountain resort. Suddenly, there appeared a man on a bicycle heading in the opposite direction. One of the women called out to the man on the bicycle, "Sir, I know you are not from this area, and you are not familiar with all the dangers around here. Please turn around because there is a road out up ahead and it's very dangerous." The man gave the woman a blank stare and continued in the direction he was going. The woman became very concerned for the man's safety, and with a louder, more intense tone, she yelled, "Please stop! Turn around! It's getting late, and you won't be able to see!"

The man became agitated, and in a curt tone, he quipped, "I can take care of myself. Mind your own business."

The woman on the other side of the road spoke up and said, "Pay no attention to her. I'm sure you'll be fine. Enjoy your ride."

The headlines from the newspaper the next morning read: "**Out-of-Town Man Plummets to Death.**" My question is this: Which of the two women showed true love and concern for the man?

What many view as narrow-minded, bigoted, hateful speech is actually great love and concern for the many who are going the wrong way. If you are heading the wrong way, opposite of God's will and direction, the way contrary to the Bible, ***PLEASE STOP! AND TURN AROUND!***

Chapter 9

What's in Your Hand?

When God called Moses to be His representative to lead the children of Israel out of Egypt, Moses said, "Who am I that I should go to Pharaoh, and that I should bring the Children of Israel out of Egypt?" So He (God) said, "I will certainly be with you" (Exodus 3:11–12).

Then Moses answered and said, "But suppose they will not believe me or listen to my voice; suppose they say, 'The LORD has not appeared to you.'" So the Lord said to him, "What is that in your hand?" And he said, "A rod" (Exodus 4:1). The word of God goes on to say that God turned that rod into a serpent when He told Moses to cast it on the ground. That rod was used many times for miracles to demonstrate that God was partnering with Moses to accomplish great results. A few other examples of the Lord using what was in someone's hand are as follows:

Jesus said to them, "How many loaves do you have?" and they said, "Seven, and a few little fish." So He commanded the multitude to sit down on the ground. He (Jesus) took the seven loaves and the fish and gave thanks, broke them and gave them to His disciples; and the disciples gave to the multitude. So they all ate and were filled, and they took up seven large baskets full of the fragments that were left. Now those who ate were four thousand men, besides women and children (Mathew 15:34–38).

There was the boy with loaves and fish: There is a lad here who has five barley loaves and two small fish, but what are they among so many? Then

Jesus said, "Make the people sit down." Now there was much grass in the place. So the men sat down, in number about five thousand. Jesus took the loaves, and when He had given thanks, He distributed them to the disciples, and the disciples to those sitting down: and likewise of the fish, as much as they wanted. When they were filled, He said to His disciples, "Gather up the fragments that remain, so that nothing is lost." Therefore, they gathered them up and filled twelve baskets with the fragments of the five barley loaves that were left over by those who had eaten (John 6:9–13).

There was also Elijah and the widow: Then the word of the LORD came to him, saying, arise, go to Zarephath, which belongs to Sidon, and dwell there. See, I have commanded a widow there to provide for you. So he arose and went to Zarephath. And when he came to the gate of the city, indeed a widow was there gathering sticks. And he called to her and said, "Please bring me a morsel of bread in your hand." So she said, "As the LORD Your God lives, I do not have bread, only a handful of flour in a bin, and a little oil in a jar: and see, I am gathering a couple of sticks that I may go in and prepare it for myself and my son, that we may eat it, and die." And Elijah said to her, "Do not fear; go and do as you have said, but make me a small cake from it first, and bring it to me; and afterward make some for yourself and your son. For thus says the LORD God of Israel: 'The bin of flour shall not be used up, nor shall the jar of oil run dry, until the day the LORD sends rain on the Earth.'" So she went away and did according to the word of Elijah, and she and he and her household ate for many days. The bin of flour was not used up, nor did the jar of oil run dry, according to the word of the LORD, which He spoke by Elijah (1 Kings 17: 8–16).

Then of course there is the biblical story of what David did with one little stone in his hand against Goliath. There have been many times in my life when I was faced with trusting God and His word or doing what seemed "logical." In most cases, I chose to trust God and His Word, and I can happily tell you that when I trusted Him and obeyed Him, He never let me down. He has done the miraculous every time.

At one point during a challenging financial time in my life, I was faced with a decision. I had received a notice that one of my utilities was about to be shut off. I had just received some money, and I was faced with the decision to tithe or use the money to pay the utility bill. I chose to trust God and mailed out a tithe check. The very next day, I received a check in the mail from a completely unexpected source, a check that covered my tithe and the money needed to pay the utility bill. I have many stories to tell of God's faithfulness in the area of tithing. Perhaps that will be my next book. My point is, I offered up to God what was in my hand, trusting Him first and foremost, and then He did the miraculous. So what is in your hand? What small, insignificant thing is in your hand that God can use to cause the miraculous to happen?

For me, it is this little book that you are reading. I am not an author with a journalism degree. I didn't have the opportunity to even attend college. I was kicked out of my home at the age of seventeen and left to fend for myself. God chose me to write this little book myself with all of its flaws so that He could take it, bless it, anoint it, and cause the miraculous to happen with it, all for His glory.

I'm not a public speaker. I was so shy as a child and adolescent that I forced myself to take drama in high school in an effort to come out of my shell. I hate pubic speaking. Yet God has opened doors for me to speak in churches here and in Africa. God opened a door for me to give my testimony on a television program that was broadcast to nearly every nation on the planet.

I'm not a physician, but God has healed people of cancer, broken bones, and other infirmities by using me as His tool. It is my greatest joy to go where He tells me and do what He says. God is healing people—spirit, soul, and body. He is leading people out of bondage. Seeing women set free through prayer and deliverance from years of torment because of abortion, will be particularly gratifying. Like Moses, I say, "Who am I?" Thankfully, our heavenly Father is allowing me to participate in the miraculous things He is doing. My greatest desire is to tell the world how great God and Jesus and the precious Holy Spirit are. I want to tell everyone how the Holy Trinity of Father, Son and Holy Spirit, have radically changed me for the good and how they are the source of all joy, peace, and happiness.

Again, I say to you, "Repent, for the Kingdom of Heaven is at hand." Ask Jesus to be your Lord and Savior, and ask Him to take control of your life. Follow Him, trust Him, and obey Him. Find a good Bible-preaching church. Go every Sabbath. Read God's word. Obey it. Then take whatever is in your hand, offer it to God, and watch Him perform the miraculous! I can hardly wait to see what He does with this little book!

And finally, I leave you with this: "But I want you to know, brethren, that the things which happened to me have actually turned out for the furtherance of the gospel" (Philippians 1:12).

GOD is great! And JESUS is the LORD! And the precious HOLY SPIRIT is truly the COMFORTER!

Appendix:
Lyrics for "Blessed Assurance" by Fanny J. Crosby

"Blessed Assurance"
Lyrics by Fanny J. Crosby

Verse 1

Blessed assurance, Jesus is mine!
O what a foretaste of Glory divine!
Heir of salvation, purchase of God,
Born of His Spirit, washed in His blood.

This is my story, this is my song,
Praising my Savior all the day long;
This is my story, this is my song,
Praising my Savior all the day long.

Verse 2

Perfect submission, perfect delight!
Visions of rapture now burst on my sight;
Angels descending bring from above
Echoes of mercy, whispers of love.

This is my story, this is my song,
Praising my Savior all the day long;
This is my story, this is my song,
Praising my Savior all the day long.

Verse 3

Perfect submission, all is at rest;
I in my Savior am happy and blest.
Watching and waiting, looking above,
Filled with His goodness, lost in His love.

This is my story, this is my song,
Praising my Savior all the day long;
This is my story, this is my song,
Praising my Savior all the day long.

Author Note

Kate Armstrong is available for ministry and can be reached at kate4minstry@hotmail.com or PO Box 877, Dana Point, CA 92629.

You can also find her on Facebook.

My testimony appeared on John Hagee Ministries telecast on May 15, 2011, and November 27, 2011.

All Bible references are from the NKJV.

Reference to GOD, JESUS, and the HOLY SPIRIT has been capitalized out of love, honor, and respect.